I0178072

ME MOTIVATED!

CHANGE YOUR LIFE IN 30 DAYS

ME MOTIVATED!

CHANGE YOUR LIFE IN 30 DAYS

© 2011 Therese Ross Brooklyn, NY

All rights reserved.

No part of this book may be reproduced or transmitted in any form or by any means without written permission from the author.

ISBN 978-0-9835296-1-3

It's not the strongest species that survives, it's not even the most intelligent that survives, it is the one most responsive to change.

CHARLES DARWIN

I dedicate this book to my daughter. If it were not for you coming into my life, I would probably still be wandering around aimlessly.

Maija, you are my everything and I hope that it is no secret to you how much I love you. I thank you for putting up with me and all that comes along with me. Thank you for being the best daughter anyone could ever ask for.

TABLE OF CONTENTS

HAVE A GREAT DAY!   3

NEW YEAR...NEW YOU???   5

GOAL!!!   7

WHAT IS YOUR DEFINITION OF SUCCESS?   9

FOCUS FOCUS FOCUS   11

IT AIN'T TOO LATE   13

TAKE OWNERSHIP OF YOUR GIFT!   15

OUTTA CONTROL...   17

WHO GOT NEXT??   19

BEFORE YOU DECIDE NOT TO VOTE...   21

WHAT ARE YOU THANKFUL FOR?   23

THE CELEBRATION   25

MOTIVATIONAL TRACKS   27

INTRODUCTION

Me Motivated! *Change Your Life in 30 Days* is designed to help you reclaim your life. It has been said that if you do something for 30 days, it becomes a habit!

Use this as a guide to develop a new way of thinking, develop a new perspective, - a new attitude.

In this book there are twelve chapters, one for each month. Use the affirmations at the end of each chapter for the entire month, say it to yourself every day, more than once a day. Use the extra space at the end of each month to make notes of what stood out in the reading for you, or something that you want to change about yourself and read that aloud every day also Make note of what you've read and how it applies to your life today. Go back at the end of the month to whatever you have written, and note how you have changed or your life has changed because of your monthly exercise.

Let me share with you what has worked for me as we come together on this journey to a better life.

Live the life you want and deserve!

ME MOTIVATED!

CHANGE YOUR LIFE IN 30 DAYS

Have A Great Day!

Have you ever had a morning when you woke up feeling just downright yucky...you had an attitude toward everything and everyone for no apparent reason?

Well my friend, even before we are totally awake, the enemy is busy planting deceiving thoughts in our mind. He wants us to feel hopeless, helpless and negative. To have a bad attitude, be selfish, self-centered, full of hatred, bitter, doubtful and fearful. Some folks call it waking up on the wrong side of the bed; I call it enemy interference.

So how do we overcome enemy interference, you ask? I am so glad you asked...we can take 15 minutes in the morning to pray, read a scripture, and reaffirm our faith in ourselves , this will enable us to have a better outlook on our day and overcome enemy interference.

Psalm 118:24 *(KJV) This is the day which the Lord hath made; we will rejoice and be glad in it.*

AFFIRMATION

I WILL HAVE A GREAT DAY!

New Year...New You???

The fireworks have been fired and the horns have been blown issuing in yet another New Year...But what will make this year different for you? What were your resolutions? Perhaps you wanted to lose weight, or stop smoking/drinking, be a better parent or maybe just be a better you.

I have listed below what should be your core values, these are the first steps to becoming a better you, a better mother, wife, husband, sister, co-worker, etc... Apply them to your everyday life and watch how it changes things.

Love:

LOVE GOD...LOVE YOURSELF!!!
Everyone else is 2nd...you got it?! Good let's move on.

Forgive:

You holding a grudge against someone is like cutting yourself and expecting someone else to bleed...the only person you are hurting is YOU! They have gone on happily living their lives and you are spiking your blood pressure every time you hear their name...LET IT GO! No one should have that much power over you who isn't in the blessing and miracle business. Forgive others so that you can be forgiven.

Matthew 5:44 "But I tell you: Love your enemies and pray for those who persecute you."

Laugh:

How many of us know a person that never smiles or looks as though the world is sitting on their shoulders? It is so important for us to take time to laugh...because when you get right down to it, life isn't as serious as some make it out to be. *"What soap is to the body, laughter is to the soul..."* Yiddish Proverb **(thinkexist.com)**

Pray:

Pray for guidance, direction and forgiveness daily. **Jeremiah 42:3** "Pray that the Lord your God will tell us where we should go and what we should do**."**

Each new year and each new day affords us the opportunity to recreate ourselves. How can we become the best that we can be?

New Year...New Day...New You??? What will you do differently this year?

AFFIRMATION

I WILL BE THE BEST ME THAT I CAN BE

Goal!!!

What are my goals? Where do I want to end up and how do I even get there? Have you thought about them? Have you thought about how you might reach them?

Perhaps your goals might include making a salary of $200,000 per year, running your own successful business, having a family, or writing a novel, perhaps it's writing your blog every week or at least once a month, whatever your goal is do you have a plan? This is a step by step plan for you to begin recognizing your goals and planning for them.

Think about your goals. Write them down.
Write down everything you want to accomplish in this lifetime.

What steps do you take to get there
Break your list down... what do you want to accomplish in the next year, six months the next three months? Take that list and break it down into what you want to achieve in the next month. Take that list and make a daily to do list that will support you reaching your goal. Example: If you want to write a novel, you should block out time for writing every day.

Do this for each of your goals. Be realistic, if your goal is to become a nurse and you haven't begun nursing school, it will take longer than 6 months or a year, but what are some of the things you can do to reach that goal now? You can begin CPR classes, you can volunteer at a hospital or nursing home, etc...

Adjust your list as your goals broaden or change.
Sometimes while we are on the path to reaching our goals, we realize that there is more to it; we need to get more education or there are extra steps. Sometimes in the midst of obtaining that

7

goal, we stumble upon something else that we would like to explore.

Allow yourself the flexibility. Be willing to adjust your goals.

Have or develop a support group of friends and family that will encourage you to stay motivated.
Start a "Go On Girl/Boy" group, where you are all supportive of each other's goals and dreams and encourage each other on a regular basis. Meet once a month, week, bi-weekly, whatever works for the group, with like-minded achievers, to cheer each other and hold each other accountable. Share your experiences, so that you may help someone who is afraid to step out and follow their dreams..

Attend events that people in the field you have chosen might attend.

There might even be some free events in your area and field that you could attend.

Research, Research, Research
When you talk to people about what you want to do, you should know all there is to know about your field.

Hebrews 6:11 *(NIV) We want each of you to show this same diligence to the very end, in order to make your hope sure.*

AFFIRMATION

I WILL PRESS ON TO REACH MY GOAL (S)

What is Your Definition of Success?

For some, success means paying all your bills on time. For another, it could mean tithing every week, or not "maxing" out your credit cards, or it could simply mean spending more time with your family. Bottom line, success doesn't mean the same to everyone. Everyone doesn't need celebrity and fame to be considered successful.

Pray to be successful by your own definition. Commit your success to the Lord and yourself.

Don't measure your success by someone else's standard!

Proverbs 16:3 *says "Commit to the Lord whatever you do and your plans will succeed."*

AFFIRMATION

MY DEFINITION OF SUCCESS IS SPECIFIC TO ME! I FEEL SUCCESSFUL WHEN I...

SUGGESTIONS:

*Pay my bills on time * Spend time with my family * Write in my journal ***

*When I take "me" time * when I tell my family I love them**
when I live my dreams

Focus Focus Focus

I have a very close friend, actually I consider her a sister. She was an unwed teenaged mom. It was rare that you would see her without her baby, and whenever you saw them they were always neat and clean, the child was well-fed and happy. What you couldn't tell was that they were homeless!

My friend was determined to change her situation and have a better life for her child. She did everything she needed to do too; she would go to the housing agency twice a week on her days off looking for a place, and asking friends to keep an ear out for her. Eventually within a few months, she had an apartment. She never lost focus of what her dream was, a place of her own for her and her child, and she persevered until it happened.

Let me ask you a question...

Where is your focus?

When you look at the things that are dominant in your life right now, are you preparing to reach your goals or *are you wasting time*? If you are partying more than you are working, is your dream to be a promoter likely to be a reality? If you are more involved in your friend's lives than your own, is your dream to be in public relations? Your focus must follow your dream.

To follow your dream, you have to get up before others and go to bed after others, associate with people that you can learn from. Read everything you can read that will help you, it would be in your best interest to take a class or two. You must eat, sleep, breathe and pray for your goals and dreams every day.

"Obstacles are what you see when you take your eye off the prize" said Vince Lombardi, one of the most successful coaches in football history.

What do you see?

Psalm 20:4 (NIV) *May He give you the desire of your heart and make all your plans succeed.*

AFFIRMATION

I AM FOCUSED

MY EYE IS ON THE PRIZE!

It Ain't Too Late

When I was a child we used to say "Do Over"... and that meant that you got another chance at whatever you were trying to do.

Well I've come by here to tell you that you can call "*DO OVER*" whenever you want. Your life doesn't have to stay where it is.

I was watching a program on TBN and a guest was being interviewed about a book she had written. When answering one of the questions, she said **"The enemy has a way of looking at your past and convincing you that it's your future."** "WHOA!" I said when I heard that. I thought to myself, how many of us are living in the shadows of our past? How many of us think that since we came from humble beginnings that's as far as we can go? My sisters and brothers, you deserve better than whatever you've had. If you've had great - you deserve greater. If you've had good - you deserve great!

Don't be intimidated by your past. Be intrigued by your future.

2 Peter 1:3 His divine power has given us everything we need for life and godliness through our knowledge of him who called us by his own glory and goodness.

AFFIRMATION
I AM INTRIGUED BY MY FUTURE
I DESERVE THE BEST
I CAN START OVER WHENEVER I WANT
IT AIN'T TOO LATE

Take Ownership of Your Gift!

Imagine with me, if you will...

It's Christmas morning, and everyone has gathered around the tree to open presents. You look over and your child has picked up *THE* gift. The one that he offered to do extra chores for, the one that he talked about constantly, the one that he asked for over and over again, even promised to correct his poor behavior if he could just get this gift. Your child has *THIS* gift in his hands, and you sit there holding your breath, filled with excitement, anticipating the joy that he will express once he opens the gift. There's a big smile on your face as you watch him rip the paper off, piece by piece. You can see the gift peeking out through the torn paper...any minute your child will shrill with glee. Your child looks at you and you are ready to burst and he says "thanx", with the same emotion that he has when it's Monday morning and he has to get up for school. Talk about a kill joy, a let down, a disappointment...well just imagine how God feels when you downplay YOUR *spiritual* gift.

You have the gift of Exhortation/Encouragement and you don't reach out to those around you that are suffering or have lost their way and offer encouraging words...you are downplaying your gift. You have the gift of Leadership and you are *following* all of your friends afraid that if you step out on faith they will not understand, or will no longer accept you as their friend...you are downplaying your gift!

Do you know what your gifts are?

Don't denounce, deny or downplay your gifts, but instead rejoice and take ownership of them.

15

2Corinthians 9:15 - *"Thanks be to God for His indescribable gift"*

AFFIRMATION

I WILL TAKE TIME TO RECOGNIZE MY SPIRITUAL GIFTS

I REJOICE IN AND TAKE OWNERSHIP OF THE GIFTS THAT GOD HAS GIVEN ME

I WILL EMBRACE THEM AND USE THEM FOR THE GLORY OF THE LORD

Outta Control...

Matthew 6:27 says: "Who of you by worrying can add a single hour to your life?"

We have a rule, my daughter and I, you can't worry about something you have no control over. The train is late...what can you do about that? Get up earlier, take an earlier train and it won't affect you.

Too often we worry or get bent outta shape over things we can't control. She was talking about me or he was staring at me...that is out of your control.

Don't sweat the small stuff...you have better things to do with that energy anyway...don't you?

Take a moment to reflect on the things that you give your energy to that are out of your control...how could you better spend that time?

AFFIRMATION
I WILL FOCUS ON THE THINGS THAT ARE WITHIN MY CONTROL
I WILL USE MY TIME WISELY

Who Got Next??

We have our first African American President...now what? What do we do, where do we go from here? Will he be our first and only African-American President?

How many times have you heard or said "if you study hard..."? **AHA!** Our children finally have a point of reference. No longer can someone say to them *"Well President is a bit ambitious, don't you think?"*

We have a history rich with firsts, onlies, and in spite ofs...how will our children contribute? How will we help them?

We as parents, relatives, teachers, pastors, deacons, neighbors, and community members have a responsibility to our children. We have the responsibility of pushing them to greatness, to encourage them to stay focused, to assist them in their endeavors, and praise them in their achievements. If they want to be President, or want to reach higher, it is our duty to help them get there.

Who's next?

1Chronicles 12:18 *Success, success to you, and success to those who help you, for your God will help you.*

AFFIRMATION
I WILL GIVE MY CHILD (REN) EVERY OPPORTUNITY TO ACHIEVE GREATNESS

Before you decide **NOT** to vote...

Think of all the ancestors who were brought here against their will. *Think* of our uncles, grandfathers, brothers, fathers, and cousins who were lynched in America.

Think of Martin Luther King Jr, Marcus Garvey, Medgar Evers and countless others who died fighting for our equal share.

Think of all the times we've heard or said "If you go to school and apply yourself, you can be anything you want." Think of all the children who had big dreams and were told they should just be janitors or housekeepers, despite their good grades and academic achievements.

Think of your children, your families; and ask can we really afford to go on living like this? Do you envision a better future for your family? If so, make it your personal mission to get out and vote. Make it your personal mission to spread the word and get others to vote. Make it your personal mission to understand the platforms your politicians are standing on. Read all you can, ask someone you know who is very into politics. We want someone in office who knows what the struggle is about and isn't afraid to roll up his sleeves and work with the people. We want someone who understands our plight and not sweep it under the rug and act as if nothing has happened. We want someone in the White House who understands our basic needs as a person, as a family, and as a community.

African Americans once ruled nations - *think Egypt and Songhai Empire.* We owe it our future generations to vote for the person(s) that will best represent our families and the issues that affect our communities.

So before you decide not to get out and vote...I want you to *THINK*... what were my ancestors fighting for?

We can no longer afford to be silent!

AFFIRMATION
I AM NO LONGER SILENT
VOTING IS MY VOICE

What Are You Thankful For?

Take a minute to think about that. What *are* you thankful for?

Too often we focus on the negative in our lives, sometimes it feels as if it outweighs the good, but maybe we take the good for granted. We pray and we ask God to grant us the desires of our heart, and how do we repay him? By complaining? Do we even say "thank you?" It wasn't big enough, or it wasn't the right color...you know what you do.

There's a commercial on television; the mother and her three children are having dinner and the children each take turns telling the mother the good things that have happened in their day. Isn't thay a lovely tradition to follow with our families...with our God?

What are you thankful for? Perhaps it was someone's hello that was a bright spot in your day. Maybe you were able to pay off a bill, or saw someone you hadn't seen in a while. Whatever it is, big or small; honor it, embrace it thankfully and enjoy it. Start a gratitude journal and write down three things that you are grateful for, everyday...it will be a great reference on difficult days.

Give Thanks! **Psalm 100:4** *Enter his gates with thanksgiving and his courts with praise; give thanks to him and praise his name.*

AFFIRMATION

I AM THANKFUL FOR...

KEEP LISTING UNTIL YOU DECIDE IT IS TIME TO STOP...
HOW MANY THINGS ARE YOU GRATEFUL FOR TODAY?
(write down at least three for the day)

The Celebration

A few years ago, I attended a Christian conference and one of the guest speakers said something that stuck with me since then; the Lord has laid it on my heart to share with you today.

"Go where you are celebrated and not just tolerated"

Y'all don't hear me!

Have you ever seen the reception a child gives when the parent comes home after being away from them all day? The child is running and screaming with glee, arms outstretched and smiling from ear to ear. Your mate should be that excited, your best friend should be that excited, wherever you go and people claim to love you there, your reception should be similar. Far too often you see people in relationships that are less than celebratory; they are downright unhappy. Sometimes God shows us things and we don't want to believe Him, we overlook it or come up with all the reasons that God is wrong. I urge you to listen to what God is telling you...through Him is where we find our celebration.

Where's your celebration? You should settle for nothing less!!

1 Corinthians 13:4 Love is patient, love is kind. It does not envy, it does not boast, it is not proud. 5 It is not rude, it is not self-seeking, it is not easily angered, it keeps no record of wrongs. 6 Love does not delight in evil but rejoices with the truth. 7 It always protects, always trusts, always hopes, always perseveres. 8 Love never fails.

AFFIRMATION

I GO WHERE I AM CELEBRATED

Motivational Tracks

STILL BLESSING ME	*GORDON CHAMBERS*
ALWAYS BE PROUD	*GORDON CHAMBERS*
SPIRIT	*KAREN BERNOD*
DON'T YOU DARE GIVE UP	*TOTAL PRAISE LIVE*
I CAN DO ALL THINGS	*TOTAL PRAISE LIVE*

When you need an extra boost because it seems everything is working against you, these songs will help to keep you uplifted and pressing on.

All of these songs are available on ITunes...do yourself a favor and add them to your repertoire.

www.ingramcontent.com/pod-product-compliance
Lightning Source LLC
Chambersburg PA
CBHW070757050426
42452CB00010B/1872

* 9 7 8 0 9 8 3 5 2 9 6 1 3 *